WHAT PARTICIPANTS SAY ABOUT UNDERSTANDING THEIR COLORS

BUSINESS PROFESSIONAL

I had the opportunity to experience True Colours with Jessie Perez this past summer, and the experience was great! Through a series of specific, personality-related questions, I learned so much more about my temperament, as well as the temperament of those with whom I work. It helped me to understand better certain "quirks" that my co-workers have, as well as what may cause and trigger certain behaviors. Jessie did an excellent job walking our group through each of the colors and our results, and giving practical, relatable examples of how to work with directly opposing temperaments. As a leader, I recommend True Colours to managers looking to maximize their organizations, better understand conflict resolution, communicate more effectively with others, and encourage harmony amongst everyone.

CHINYERE
CHARLOTTE, NC

ARIST

I took the True Colours test, and it was one of the most valuable steps I have taken in understanding my relationships and myself with other people.

Before I participated in the workshop, I always had frustrations with my friends and loved ones because I based my expectations of them on how I thought people 'should' act, based on how 'I' would act.

The workshop helped me understand, in the simplest and most basic way possible, the differences in personality and behavior types. Now, I not only understand myself and my temperaments better, but I can better understand other people and why they act the way they do.

I had taken a bunch of other personality tests before this one, but they were more complicated and left one with an impossible combination of letters to remember. The True Colours workshop deals with four basic colors. It is extremely easy to understand, remember, and apply.

TRACY
NIGERIA, AFRICA

I took True Colours in 2015 and it has revealed to me a few things about myself. The test itself was simple to understand and the test giver (Jessie) was very patient with all of us. I enjoyed the overall experience because I did not only learn about my tendencies and characteristics but it also helped me to understand how other people think. I think that this information has helped me become more understanding of others and has helped see the reason behind people's actions. For example, I had some trouble relating to my mom and certain other people because I didn't understand them. It turns out that my mom has gold tendencies and I am a strong green (with gold being the lowest of my colors), which has helped me relate and be more understanding with my mom.

GABRIELA
COSTA RICA / NASHVILLE, TN

COLOR BY DESIGN

WHY YOU DO WHAT YOU DO,
THINK WHAT YOU THINK, AND
CARE ABOUT WHAT YOU CARE ABOUT

Color *by* Design

Jessie Lee Perez

WE SPEAK COLOR PUBLISHING

COLOR BY DESIGN

*Why You Do What You Do, Think What You Think,
and Care about What You Care About*

ISBN   978-1-5445-0071-3 *Paperback*
       978-1-5445-0072-0 *Ebook*

Contents

———

Acknowledgments

Many people contributed love, strengths, and talents to make possible this book's publication. I would like to give a special thanks to all those who supported me publicly and privately in their time and prayers. For the inspiration, opportunity, motivation and stamina I give thanks to my Creator, my God. Thanks also to Teirra Jemison Schreiner for lending her editing talents to fine tune the written text – you are priceless. Thanks to my husband, Antolino Perez Diaz, for believing in me as I pressed down the path to the finish line of this race, yet the starting line of all that this will bring. And one more special thanks to my mom who, since I was a child, always told me I could do anything I could dream.

Prologue

Where do you fit on the diversity spectrum? What color are you? How do you fit in with those around you? I am not asking about your outer appearance, I'm asking about your inner colors; the things that make you do what you do, think like you think, care about what you care about. These colors help segment society for the most complete and satisfying diversification – diversity of thought.

It cuts across all other cross-sections of diversity – culture, race, age, gender, etc.

Whether tribes in Africa, the Black-White roots of the United States, the Spanish-Indigenous people of Latin America, age and generations or even the man versus woman contrast, diversity so often divides us. If we were true to ourselves and would allow ourselves to see the greater picture, we could value the diversity for what it really is; every party bringing what each offers to the proverbial table – to create together something whole.

Without one, there is a hole, but only together are we whole.

We are designed for relationship and we are designed to create. Together a man and woman come into relationship and create a child. Together groups of people come into relationship and form a nation. Together a team comes into relationship and builds a product. Together we offer all of the pieces; together we can do more – together we accomplished the big picture.

Problems arise when someone doesn't want to engage; doesn't want to look at the bigger picture, or thinks the bigger picture should be a unity of like people and "unlike" people do not belong.

The definition however of what makes someone "unalike" has been sorely skewed since the beginning of society. People have most often used outward appearance to categorize people into groups of like and unalike. This is superficial however and lacks authenticity to define who someone is. If we were able to peel back all of the external factors and independent experiences, we would come to the fundamental core of who we are – the things that make us who we are, do what we do, think how we think, need what we need, and care about what we care about. This might be known as our temperament, and the variety of temperaments across people can actually be accurately expressed through the analogy of four colors – blue, green, orange and gold.

When we look at people for who they really are, then and only then, can we most accurately view the truest form of diversity – diversity of thought.

With this view in mind, we can finally step past diversity as a means to divide us and appropriately view diversity as a means to unite us. We need each other, and each other's strengths to complete us – to most completely create all that we are meant to create.

After reading this book, you will see yourself with a fresh sense of clarity and hopefully see all of humanity through a new set of colorful lenses.

Color does not exist except through light, so in the absence of light, colors have no value unto themselves. In such, we have little point in our own abilities without purpose. Purpose guides our abilities to have an impact; to be employed with an aim of accomplishing something of value. If we have abilities without purpose, it's equivalent to having those abilities stored in a dark closet. Having purpose provides a light to our path. God shines that light and in Him not only can we most clearly find our purpose, but that is where we can also see our truest of colors.

I love science. I love data. I love the stories it can tell us. Working at NASA as an analyst for four years, and then in the healthcare industry to help revolutionize cancer care and the ability to respond to early detection, I have learned how valuable data and science can be to mankind. The experience of discovery and being on the cutting edge of discovery is suspenseful and energizing. I have heard it said many times however, that God and science are not compatible and I think this idea is completely miss-based. Science is simply the discovery of all God has created. The more we know through science, not just hypotheses, the closer we come to understanding God Himself.

What if we were all scientifically discoverable, not just through psychology or physiology but actually logically discoverable to the innermost core of our cognitive functional design? And so we are.

As we explore the science of humanity through this book, we will also discover the heart and the content of God's very nature. Let us embark on an adventure to discover the logically ordered community of human design that has been right before our eyes all along.

THE ENCOUNTER

I stood in front of a class of 96 software professionals at an esteemed conference in Raleigh, North Carolina.

I was about to introduce them to themselves in a way that they never could have suspected. I knew that the room was mixed. Some had come hopeful to gain some value that they could take back to their organizations. Some had come skeptical but they were encouraged to attend by their organizations. Others didn't really have any expectation at all but wondered at the colorful small toys and candy strewn across many of the tables when they entered the room. As the session got started, interest quickly rose and I had the attention of the entire room. By the time we wrapped up the workshop, the participants were roaring with applause, with many coming to thank me for delivering the session. One man even told me he was my biggest fan.

What moved these people was not another fact-based talk or motivational speech, but rather interpersonal truths about themselves and those they knew that cut straight to their cores, delivered in a way that not only changed their worldview on humanity, but also gave them initial tools and a clear vision for using the insight in everyday life. They had encountered themselves through the lenses of color.

When we understand others and ourselves with the context of our own innate design in mind, so many misunderstandings fade that make way for grace and sometimes even admiration.

While this book will give you a clear view of the colors and likely a firm grasp on your brightest color. I would like to add a disclaimer: this book is not designed to take the place of a live workshop assessment for your colors, but rather to bring additional clarity and context to how we may function in our most optimal states.

TEMPERAMENT DEFINED

Now is a good time to mention that the color associations in this book are not describing personalities but rather temperament. Temperament is the fundamental cognitive design of how people are structured. This would be the "who we are" deep into the core, from birth to death.

Personality, however, is the combination of temperament and life experience. Personality is fluid and can theoretically change over time based on events, experiences, and worldview.

Temperament is a topic that has a record of exploration back to the time of Hippocrates. Many scientists have studied it and have produced various tools in an attempt to explain it, a few of whom are Carl Jung and Myers/Briggs. True Colours (yes, the spelling is correct) is not new content, as it is based on the same discoveries as its predecessors, only it is further simplified into just four colors.

These colors work together to make up a person's color spectrum. No person is a single color, but rather a mix of all four colors with varying degrees of brightness. The brightest color in a person's spectrum is going to be the color with which a person naturally leads. This is also the color with which the person needs his or her needs to be met in order to operate in his or her very best form. The second brightest color in each person's spectrum will influence the brightest color in a variety of circumstances. The paler colors are not necessarily out of the scope of influence, though the more pale a color falls on the color spectrum, the more difficult it is to employ that color.

INTERACTIVE DOMINANCE EXERCISE

We are about to explore the colors themselves to get a better understanding and give context to the content of the spectrum. Before we do that however, I'd like you to perform a very brief exercise. Take now a pen and a piece of paper.

On your paper, hold the pen in your dominant hand and apply your signature to the center of the page. Sign it as if you were signing a simple document.

Now, take the pen in your less dominant hand and just below the first signature sign your name again in the same way.

How did that feel? Was it awkward? Less comfortable? Difficult? Did it look as good? Did it take a little longer? Maybe a lot longer?

This is kind of the same as using your paler, or less dominant, colors. You can do it, though it may not look as good, feel as good or be as easy.

Don't let this discourage you. Thankfully, the world is full of people composed of all different spectrum strengths. This means that in areas you may struggle, there is someone else out there that excels in that very area. It is not a competition and you don't need to struggle to keep up, but rather learn to partner with the counterpart of your area of weakness.

When we partner with people who complement our strengths and weaknesses, we maximize everyone's greatest ability for the best result. Human beings are designed for relationships; perhaps we are wired with shortcomings just to have to partner with others to help fill our gaps.

Could it be that our weaknesses are not a deficit of strength, but rather a part of the intentional **design**?

There is only one who excels in all four areas and that is God, the Creator, Himself. He is 100% of each color. Yes, I know, for all of you math savvy people, that doesn't seem to add up, but let me equate it to a father to help give you a contextual example from which to pull.

When a man has a son, the man can be considered 100% a father, he either is or he is not, he can't be halfway a father, or 30% a father. However, that same man was birthed by someone, so that also makes him 100% a son, again no partial here. So, essentially that makes the man both 100% a father and 100% a son, depending on the role in perspective.

While we will only ever be a spectrum of parts, God is the whole, thus in whatever area we lack, we can partner with Him and He can sufficiently fill the gap.

CHAPTER 1

Colors

———

Let's talk color.

Now, let's talk about the colors themselves. Orange, Blue, Gold, and Green are the four colors that make up every person's spectrum.

As a brief overview, Orange is the adventurous, risks tolerant type, while Blue is characterized by its need for connectedness and to be helpful. Gold is by far the most organized and structured of the colors, and Green is highlighted by the logical and big picture visionary way of thinking.

All of these colors are valuable and there is no color that is better than any other color. None of the colors need fixing. They are what they are and there are positives and negatives to each. I will call these the bright sides and the shadows as I discuss each color in more detail.

You may have already begun to guess and self-assess what your brightest color is just from the brief description of each, though I expect the facts will become clearer as you continue to read. Keep in mind that you could potentially see a little bit of yourself in all the colors since we are all made up of a spectrum. More than likely one or two colors will begin to emerge more dominantly as you explore each color in greater detail.

ORANGE

Let's start things off with Orange, since people of orange dominance like to go first – yes, I said it out loud, and while there will be absolutely no color bashing, there will be a little gentle color teasing here and there. I hope you brought your good sense of humor.

If you are good at getting speeding tickets, or are that person in the group who actually likes change, or if you've ever been known to say (or think) "you're not the boss of me" – you might be an Orange.

I remember as a child my step sister shouting out that last phrase on a number of occasions. As she grew up, she had the need to have adrenaline pumping through her veins and still does. She works as a dog musher in the eco-adventure world of Colorado. She is currently out touring the European landscape during the off-season and I'm sure her adventures won't end there. If any of this sounds like fun to you, you may have an influencing orange hiding in the wings even if it isn't your brightest color.

Oranges have a need for freedom. While this can look a little different from person to person, the essence is the same. They don't want to be put in a box, made to follow a routine over and over the same way, or micromanaged. They need to feel some autonomy in decision-making and to an Orange, change isn't only welcomed, it's necessary. Oranges also have an attraction to fun. Fun can make something worth doing in its own right. Oranges also tend to like to be out in front and will often be the life of the party in one way or another. Often times Oranges tend to be talkers and may have gotten into trouble as a child for disrupting class.

Oranges also happened to be rule-breakers. They just are – they can't help it. They don't have to break it a lot, just a little will do. You've likely heard the phrase, "rules are made to be broken," well I can pretty much guarantee that was coined by a bright Orange.

I, being a Green-Orange myself, have a considerable influence of orange on my green. As such, I've spent a fair amount of time adventuring in other countries and taking risks. Interestingly enough, it doesn't matter from what cultural background someone comes, the wiring as described by the colors still applies.

As I was visiting in-laws in Guatemala, I had gone fishing one day. The heat and physical exertion expended left me with severe heat exhaustion. The next day while cooking, I simply was not in the mood to have seven nieces, nephews, and sibling in-laws, all under the age of 10, scurrying around me. I usually let them watch and help in the kitchen as I cooked, but this day I established a rule. I used the tiles on the floor to create an imaginary boundary and told them that they could only come as far as one tile length into the kitchen, but no further than that line. This went well until my little niece Haydi arrived. When she first entered the house, she stood in line with all the other children, watching from a distance. She had not been there when I set the rule. The moment she discovered there was a rule however, everything changed. I turned around to find her just over the line, turned facing the other children and pointing to the line that she had crossed to tell them that there was a line that they could not cross. I scolded her, pointing out that she was over the very line at which she was pointing. She quickly crossed back over the line and stood with the other children. Only moments later however, she was right back over that line, again, pointing out to the other children the line they could not cross. Again, I scolded her, this time with the warning that if she could not stay behind the line, not only would she be out of the kitchen, but she would be out of the house as well. That's right, moments later she was over the line and out of the house. It's quite amazing how certain aspects of who we are can show up so clearly even as children. Haydi was not trying to be a disobedient child; she just had an internal need to cross the line – most literally.

BLUE

My young sister-in-law Jasmi, from the same group of children in our Guatemalan kitchen, is very blue. While I've yet to discover clearly her other influencing colors, her blue shines through brightly. She is always willing to and ready to help and she's the first to be at someone's side if the person is hurt or ill. She is commonly found trying to teach someone something, or pretending to be the mommy or caregiver to small animals on the community farm. She has an innate sense of compassion and empathy – all Blues do. It's something that just comes naturally to them; they can't help it. If you need someone to come cry with you, call a Blue; seriously.

Blues have an innate sense of connectedness. They look out for others. There's a book called Ruth. This book recounts the life of a young widow and her mother-in-law, to whom she pledges her life commitment even though her husband, the woman's son, has died. Through the story, we meet a very wealthy man named Boaz. He is a slightly older man, but an eligible bachelor nonetheless. Evident even in his position of power and wealth, it is clear that his heart is compassionate towards those who work in his fields. Upon discovering that Ruth has been following behind his workers picking up the remnants of what they were harvesting, not only does he not reprimand her for taking from his field, but he actually tells her to continue to take from his field and not go to someone else's field. He encourages her to go out with the ladies he employs and instructs the young men not to touch her.

As the course of the book goes, he makes no advances on her but continues to show her kindness. After a time she makes it known that she favors him. He is honored, but knows that another man has claimed her, though she has not gone after any of the young man around. In taking the other man into consideration, he approaches him to see if he has any intent towards Ruth. The man knows that if he commits to taking Ruth as his wife he would have to uphold her former husband's inheritance and forego his own inheritance. This is something he isn't willing to do. Having settled the intent, Boaz returns to Ruth and takes her as his wife. (Book loosely paraphrased from NASB)

In this story, we see Boaz' kindness and compassion for Ruth, a pretty young lady, but we also see that he is intent in looking out for another man for whom he is not responsible. I would venture to say that Boaz may have been a valiant example of a blue gentleman. Don't mistake a Blue's softness for weakness. As we can see through the example of Boaz, he commanded respect and lived as a person of authority, yet doing it all through a lens of compassion.

Blues have a need to be appreciated and they value authenticity. They tend to make excellent mentors and value relationships as one of the most important things in life. For Blues, family is very important, but "family" is not necessarily defined by blood. A Blue may consider unrelated people family. But not all blood relatives may be counted in as family. It's a relational connection more than a contextual connection. And once someone is "out" for Blue, it is extremely hard to get back in. Blues will forgive, once, twice, but do it again and it's "no blue for you."

GOLD

Let's go next to Gold. As with precious metals, we find Gold people also extremely valuable. It is the gold behind most administrative structure, accounting, and a variety of other needed infrastructure in the world today. They keep us in line and on time.

Golds tend to be extremely organized. They often make a list for everything and there is no better feeling for Gold than checking something off that list. Gold may even add something to a list that has already been completed if it wasn't on the list originally, just to check it off and get credit for it. They want that "completed" list.

Golds tend to have a strong work ethic and take their responsibility very seriously. Work is important to Gold. Golds also tend to be worriers. They worry about every-thing – you can't tell gold "don't worry," it's like telling water not to be wet – it's simply a component of who they are.

Golds like to have a plan, and stick to the plan in all ways possible. They don't like last-minute changes and prefer to operate in an environment of stability. Routine is good for Golds. Consistency is a place of peace. Golds also value family and friends, but unlike Blues, they are more formal in their relationship context. The heart of family for Gold is based in heritage, lineage, and tradition. Friends are fine, but they're not looked at the same way as family.

Golds also have a strong sense of right and wrong and for them there is little gray area. They tend also to hold ideals, which can make them less accepting of alterna-tive options and views. Golds can often be leaned on as a strong moral compass.

While gold people may not be the adventurous sort, unless of course they have an orange influence of sub-stantial weight, the value they bring to the human race is unmeasurable.

Just recently, I had scheduled to do an abbreviated

workshop for my grandparents and aunt and uncle in preparation for a talk I was giving in the area near where they live. While in casual conversation at the dinner table the evening before the workshop, my grandfather referred to things being in their place and how there should be a place for everything and everything should be in its place.

I had to smile. In that one statement, he confirmed all my suspicions. Sure enough, the next day's workshop revealed that he was a bright Gold. A phrase that rings true to the core of Gold, "a place for everything and everything in its place." When things are in order, Gold can have peace. Structure provides security.

GREEN

Now on to Green. A Green would be the least likely to have picked up this book in the first place, as for a Green the skepticism may have crept in asking the question, "why does this matter?" which I would like to point out is the very topic of the next chapter "Why this matters".

Greens are very logically driven. If something makes sense, it's in, if it doesn't, it's out. Unfortunately, emotions are often left in the "it doesn't make sense" category. Being a bright Green myself, I can see the value this can bring in some situations, but also the insensitivity it can impose upon others in situations that may warrant more emotional involvement.

Greens like to get straight to the point, without a lot of fluff. They give communication that way and they prefer to get communication in the same way. Greens look for the "why" in things. "Why does this work like this?" "Why is that made like that?" "Why do I have to do that?" These are just a few examples. Bright green people may have gotten into trouble at school or home as a child for asking why. This questioning may have been interpreted as rebelliousness. Actually, however, Greens have an innate need to know "why." Greens are lifetime learners. They are always gleaning more information and looking things up. I've asked many Greens in my workshops the same question, "what would happen if someone told you that you could never learn another new thing again?" I receive the same answer every time. It's always something along the lines of "I'd die."

Greens tend naturally to be able to see the big picture in a situation and can quickly see how all of the components fit together. While a Green may not want to know all the individual details of a job or product, he or she will see the greater direction of impact for those components. Greens tend to look at things from the 10,000 foot view.

Greens tend to respect competency in others. If someone conveys a level of proficiency in a task or job, then a Green will expect that person to do a good job at what the person is tasked to do. There is little room for error or incompleteness in the Green's expectation for this person. However, if a person indicates that he or she is novice or in training or is the first day on the job, then the Green has sufficient grace for that person to make errors or need correction. Once a person has lost the respect of a Green however, is extremely difficult to earn it back.

While a Green may appear to express extremely high expectations, one thing is certain; Greens will never hold anyone to a higher standard than to the standard they hold themselves.

CHAPTER 2

Why This Matters

___

COMMUNICATION SUCCESS

Why do True Colours matter? What if True Colours could make you more successful? That of course, would depend on your definition of success and what makes that up. Do you define success as more consistently accurate products, more harmonious relationships, missions that are more productive, greater peace in life, ability to influence, or maybe acceptance? Whatever it is that resonates with you in regards to success, there is likely a way that True Colours can positively drive you towards it.

Understanding your colors and the colors of those around you is crucial in optimizing communication, and optimized communication is crucial to the success of projects, programs, and missions. When we take into consideration the needs, values and strengths of others we reduce misunderstandings and optimize opportunities.

Oftentimes communication is thought of simply as the words that we speak, however, communication also includes the method in which we deliver the communication, the tone we use, the amount of words, and the context of those words, as well as any additional body language.

OFFICE LANGUAGE SCENARIO

Let's use an example of two co-workers sitting in an office space and one coworker wants to invite the other one to a meeting.

For the first example, our two co-workers will be Gold and Blue. The Gold coworker is sitting only just across from the Blue coworker and sends an email to the Blue coworker requesting the Blue's attendance to a meeting at 2 P.M. for important updates that need to be discussed. The Blue co-worker receives the email and rather than simply replying accept or decline, the Blue coworker is offended. Why is this?

Since Blues tend to be very relational, it could come across harsh and cold to a Blue for an email to be sent as the only means of communication when the co-worker was within speaking range in the same room. The proper means of communication the Blue would have expected would have been simply for the Gold to turn around and speak to the Blue regarding the meeting and then an email would have been fine for follow-up, but certainly not for as the entire means of communication.

In response to the e-mail, a Blue may turn around and say, "Okay, thanks, see you then." That might be the end of the communication from the Blue. The Gold then might be offended because the Blue didn't take the time to accept the meeting because for Gold, that is the proper thing to do.

In this case, there are now two co-workers that have both been offended by the other, not because either did anything wrong, but simply because their expectations regarding the methods of communication were contrary. How could this have been handled better?

If both the Gold and the Blue understood each other's needs then the Gold could have sent the email and followed it up with, "by the way I just sent you an email regarding a meeting I like you to attend." The Blue then could have responded "thanks" and then followed that up with an acceptance of the meeting.

In doing so, both parties would have had their communication needs met with respect to their primary colors and neither party would have been offended, making for a much better working environment.

Had an Orange been one of the members of this example,

both communications by verbal means and by written means would have been welcomed. The preference would have been for a different reason than the Blue and Gold however. An Orange would have appreciated the verbal communication since Oranges tend to like things on the spot and on the fly, in an in-person way. However, an Orange would have also appreciated a written form of communication because they tend to forget things once they hear them and their focus passes on to a new topic.

Had a Green been party to this example, the Green would have preferred a simple calendar invite with basic information regarding the intent of the meeting. This would have put a direct link to their calendar. This way the calendar invite is there to remind them. It is short, efficient, and no further discussion is needed.

We can see from this one example how communication, both the method as well as potentially the words, tone, and other factors, can completely change the effectiveness of teamwork. Imagine how much more so across an entire team.

RELATING TO OTHERS

We are created with areas of strength and areas of weakness. But, why do we have weaknesses? The simple answer is because no one is perfect, thus the deficit is what remains as our weaknesses. But, what if that's not really the answer? What if we are made with weaknesses as an intentional part of the design rather than the empty spot that isn't filled with strength? What if the weaknesses were created with just as much thought and purpose as the strengths?

Weaknesses make us reliant upon others. They ensure that we can't do everything ourselves. We are built and designed to be in relationship; relationship with each other and relationship with God. In order to ensure the fostering of relationships, particularly among people for whom relationships are not strengths, each person has a set of strengths that perfectly fits into the space of some-one else's weaknesses.

I was talking to someone recently who said he doesn't have any friends and he doesn't need any. He said it doesn't bother him; he just doesn't connect with people. There are a couple colors where it may be more likely for some-one to say something like this – namely Green and Gold. My response to this person was that "we are designed to have friends and that without anyone, if we fall; there is no one there to pick us up."

I explained that oftentimes friends can develop through very practical means. Maybe two people can mutually benefit each other; maybe it's not even a benefit that exists currently, but just the potential that one could exist in the future. Keep in touch with these people, for you never know when one of your strengths could fill that person's weakness for a season or for a particular need, and vice versa.

"Friendship doesn't just happen. We choose our friends. And either consciously or unconsciously, we choose them on the basis of need and hunger." (Les Giblin, *How to Have Confidence and Power in Dealing with People*, pp.61)

I would recommend reading chapter 6 of Les Giblin's book for greater insight on making friends if this might be something you'd like to explore further.

Granted, there are some people that maybe you've really made an effort and you just don't click with them. That's okay, let them go. No hard feelings, as there is not enough time in the day to be friends with everyone. Out of some of the associations true friendship will develop. There are different levels of relationships and for different seasons.

Some people are only meant to be in your life for a season or for a particular purpose or event. Some people are designed for the long term. Some people only ever get to the introductory-level, while others may eventually get to the deep friend level. Whatever the role is for someone in your life, you have little control over that. However, it is your responsibility to take the initial steps and appropriate follow-up steps needed to allow the relationship to blossom where it will.

People naturally connect more easily with people who are like themselves. While we may more easily find things to talk about when the things that we respect and motivate us are similar, it is not uncommon to find ourselves attracted, not necessarily in the romantic sense, although that is common as well, to people who fill areas of our weakness. Perhaps, we may subconsciously recognize some qualities and skills that we interpret as positive that we lack.

While we may choose our friends, not all relationships are initiated by selective choice. Some relationships begin because people are co-workers hired by the same company, or are roommates, or otherwise connected through a means of role or responsibility. Interestingly, highly successful people will often seek out relationships with people who have areas of strength that counter their own gaps. They understand the value in maximizing one's strengths and partnering with others who have strengths in their area of weaknesses, rather than just surrounding themselves with people who are just like themselves.

I've met numerous spouses who discover after participating in a True Colours workshop that they are opposites in spectrum. This often surprises them but it makes sense that someone might be attracted to someone of opposite spectrum for any of three reasons.

1. Subconsciously realizes that this person has strengths that fill their areas of weakness
2. Finds the actions/experiences (that are driven by underlying colors) of the other person different and fascinating as compared to the person's own experiences
3. Admires qualities that the person him or herself lacks

While not everyone marries a spouse with contrasting colors, there have been many examples of this occurring. There have also been many times in a workshop that spouses have come to forgiveness of their spouses. Eventually realizing that they truly think quite differently from one another and no harm was intended.

Not only have spouses come to forgiveness, but other people as well. In one workshop a woman shared what I like to call an "ah-ha" moment. That's the moment when the lights come on and the concepts really connect with the person. She started by announcing that she had some apologies to make. From there she elaborated that she and her sister had not invited their cousin anywhere in nearly thirty years.

You see, this woman, I'll call her Melanie, was a bright

Gold. She was a fantastic project manager within her organization and planning was a natural, and necessary, part of her life. From her story, I gathered that her sister was also quite Gold. Her cousin, however, was a shining Orange. As she explained her revelation, she told of how her cousin on several occasions had invited her and her sister on trips. She would tell them that they would be going in just a couple of weeks. The sisters quickly decided that their cousin really didn't want them to go since she gave them no time to plan. Of course, the clincher to their assumption was the couple of times that they had invited her to go do things with them and gave her plenty of notice, nearly a year in advance, yet their cousin's response was, "I don't even know if I'll be alive in a year." So, Melanie and her sister concluded that certainly she didn't want to go with a response like that, so they stopped inviting her.

Bright Oranges live each day as it comes, it's all about the here-and-now for Orange, and about the fun that can be had – after all, tomorrow is not promised, right? For Golds however, not planning and taking the care to look at the future and try to plan for the unexpected and the expected alike is simply irresponsible and who would want to be irresponsible, right? As different as these two ways of thinking are, neither is right or wrong, they're just different. Without understanding the way in which the other one thinks, it makes it easy to disregard the other as ridiculous or even harbor resentment against the person. That day, Melanie came to a place of forgiveness. Not only did she learn to understand better herself and others, but also she walked out of that room with a sense of freedom she would have never experienced if she had never understood the perspective of her cousin.

A TALE OF FORGIVENESS

I myself have come to forgiveness through the understanding of how True Colours applies to the people in my life. I want to tell you a little about my stepmother. She came into our lives when I was six years old. When I was a child, I used to think that she was very mean. We never seemed to see anything from the same perspective and I remember how I would think she was so rigid and controlling.

My brightest colors are Green-Orange, in that order, but as a child, I had few responsibilities, so my Green had little opportunity to shine to all its glory. While my color arrangement didn't change, my influencing Orange took every opportunity to fill the gap. My stepmother however, I now realize is very Gold. While she has not taken the assessment as of yet, her "tells" are hard to hide. We were truly on opposite ends of the color spectrum.

Not only have I come to forgive her for what I now understand as just her being her, but I also can appreciate her strengths and see how they have both influenced me and improved me in several ways. My favorite way is her use of lists for everything. She literally had a "get ready" list posted in the hall near the bathroom that listed every single thing we, the children, were supposed to do prior to walking out the door to go to school. It was detailed line by line. I look back on that now and wonder how my orangeness ever got off to school without it.

SHEDDING COLOR ON HUMANITY

Understanding humanity through the lens of color has not only helped me forgive others, but it has also helped me to realize that I have been insensitive to others. My mother, who raised us most of the time, is very Blue. While her brightest color is actually Orange, her Blue very strongly influences her Orange. I, being very Green however, now see how I have made her life very difficult at times, and I was completely oblivious to it until I discovered myself through True Colours. I then began to see how others saw me. I like to get right to the point and tell it how I see it. That way of communication just seems to make sense to me. My mother however, as do all Blues, expects to give and receive information and communication with much softer edges. There have been a few times even now that stand out in my mind when I thought I was doing her a favor and being helpful in my assessment of the situation but rather I made her cry. It breaks my heart looking back on it, though I truly didn't understand it at the time.

It's easy and natural for us to operate only in the context and framework in which we ourselves are wired and designed. We think that everyone thinks as we do and should understand things from the same context we do. When we begin however to understand the four main temperament types and consider how people from those temperaments unlike our own think and the perspective from which they see things, it will forever change our outlook on humanity.

CHAPTER 3

External Forces on Our Colors

———

HOW SITS ON WHOM...

Our colors are like our foundation, the most fundamental core of who we are and what makes us tick. This is not the whole of our makeup however. If we were to evaluate ourselves starting at the outside and continue to peel away the layers of how we are and what makes us who we are, we would ultimately strip down to our colors and that is where we would find that there is nothing else left to peel away. While True Colours will continuously prove accurate, there are external forces that can throw off the "tells" for certain people. As we look further at the factors that lay on top of our colors, we will be able to understand how those apply. The colors are "who" we are. Everything else lay on top of that and creates the "how" we are.

Who vs. How

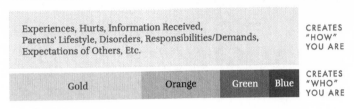

| Experiences, Hurts, Information Received, Parents' Lifestyle, Disorders, Responsibilities/Demands, Expectations of Others, Etc. | CREATES "HOW" YOU ARE |

| Gold | Orange | Green | Blue | CREATES "WHO" YOU ARE |

Image 1: Original design by Jessie Lee Perez for *Color By Design*

Sometimes these factors that lay on top may influence the "how" we are, and potentially make it challenging for others to clearly identify the tells with full accuracy, but this overlay will never change the "who" we are.

The "how" we are can be changed, but the "who" we are is always going to be who we are. Your personality may adapt over time and experience, but your temperament will still drive the most essential parts of who you are.

HOW DO EXTERNAL FORCES WEIGH IN?

The facts of who we are will not change, but there are external forces that can throw off the "tells" for certain people, making it more challenging to accurately assess the person's colors.

I have a former roommate who is a great example of how the "tells" of others can be misleading due to external overlay. I lived with a young lady; we'll call her Kelly, for a while and we became friends through the process. Kelly was in town visiting one summer a few years after we'd been roommates. She agreed to participate in a True Colours session. I thought for sure I knew her colors. She was going to be Orange/Blue. I was so confident of this that I wrote it on a piece of paper and had it ready so that after the session I could pull it out just show how well I knew her. Well, I could not have been much more wrong. Kelly turned out to be a Gold/Blue. I asked her how that could be, as she behaved so much like an Orange? She confirmed that she certainly did a lot of Orange things, but that her needs and values fully aligned with Gold. The assessment had told it as it was. After talking further it soon became apparent why she seemed so Orange when clearly she was Gold. Kelly has a textbook Attention Deficit Disorder (ADD) condition, likely the strongest case I've ever seen, and having been challenged with it myself, I know it well. What had occurred is that the symptoms of ADD were overlaying her temperament and making her do Orange-looking things when in fact she was Gold.

- Tactile things were very common in her life – she like to have things in her hands that she could touch or play with. This is very common for Oranges.
- Her lack of focus on any one thing for too long – another common Orange characteristic.
- Her desire to be active and outside, riding bikes, hiking, camping, etc. – certainly another common Orange tell.

There were numerous other things that had made me think Orange, when in actuality; the ADD was acting as a film or veil over her true temperament as far as the external display of her actions.

While it proved difficult for me to pick up on her "tells" accurately, this may actually work to her advantage in some ways. She may become more relatable to Oranges even though she doesn't actually think as they do. It also provides her a little more flexibility in life than would typically be common in Golds. This also can provide an additional challenge for her however, in that some of the very thing she does due to her ADD that look Orange, are the very things that bring stress to Gold.

Other examples of overlay could include Obsessive-Compulsive Disorder (OCD) that may present false tells of a Gold dominance, masking as order, structure and repetition. Some lighter levels of the autism spectrum could also masquerade as Green, with examples to include being awkward in social situations, stating communication directly, and not taking into consideration the possible emotional impact to others.

I will add also that there are likely people throughout the world that may falsely believe they exhibit levels of disorders, such as those common on the autism spectrum or in ADD, but in actuality they are simply very bright in a particular color (Green or Orange respectively for example) and have never been shown how to operate within this cognitive framework.

Other examples of overlay that could impact a person's tells include past hurts, responsibilities, previous experiences, the expectations of others, and several other factors. Another layer that sits on top of the colors is the introvert/extrovert component.

While the Introvert/Extrovert component is another overlay and is not part of the color spectrum, some predecessor temperament assessments have included it as a core component of the results output. It is more appropriate to assess this component separately. Some people have asked if it is possible to have an introverted Orange or an extroverted Gold – the answer – absolutely. How does that look? An introvert is harder to tell but still has the same needs. An extrovert still thinks in accordance with the particular color spectrum, but may be more likely to exhibit outwardly the brightest colors. Essentially, while the introvert/extrovert component typically influences demeanor, this is more about from where a person draws refreshment. An introvert is reenergized in alone time, while an extrovert is reenergize in the company of others.

Anytime we operate outside of our innate colors, we are challenged. If you recall the signature exercise using your non-dominant hand, it is a figurative example of the elements of stress that can be caused when we are acting and responding outside of the context of our truest colors.

There is another overlay that can actually bring up some of our weaknesses into a balanced-looking state however, and that is the overlay of God. It is possible through the grace of God to operate in the form of a less dominant color without the elements of stress that naturally occur otherwise. While people in the church-world tend to throw around the phrase "through the grace of God," I mean it in the most literal sense. The closer we are in a relationship with God, the more He, and His character, is overlain on us. Since He is 100% of every color that means that He can fill whatever gaps we may have in the way of weakness. This also means that He can optimize our strengths. Every color has a bright side and a shadow side, so each color has tendencies that might be considered less desirable by the general populace when exhibited. When God overlays us, He can turn the light on over the shadows; the perfection of His color can lift our shadowed tendencies and release more of the bright side through us. A Green for example when applying logic to a solution may also apply logic to how best to communicate the solution in a way that the rest of the group would positively respond. In a natural setting, a Green would just come with the solution in the most direct and factual means without forethought of how the other people involved might perceive the communication. If the Green has not been trained in this and the person has a growing and healthy relationship with God, he or she may see this unnatural overlay come through in situations and might clearly be able to identify it as outside of his or her normal manner of conduct and thought.

I have personally seen Blue shine through me in a situation and was in awe as I experienced it occurring. As I witnessed this within myself, I knew clearly that it wasn't naturally from me but rather God filling my weakness with His Blue and compassion.

Whatever area you may lack, you can rest in God to fill in the difference if you are in a relationship with Him and are willing to let Him inside. There is a scripture that says, "My grace is sufficient for you, for my power is made perfect in weakness" (2 Corinthians 12:9). No greater is there an example than this.

Example:

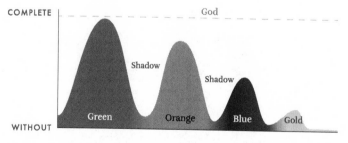

Image 2: Original design by Jessie Lee Perez for *Color By Design*

This is an illustration of what it might look like visually. Since we are all a mixture of all colors to some level, no one can ever be completely without any one color. And since our total of colors, makes up 100% of us, and no color can be 0%, then it is also true that we cannot in ourselves ever be 100% in any color either. This means that in and of ourselves, we can never be fully optimized in any color.

While the total of all four colors makes up 100% of who we are, the True Colours assessment scoring system is based on a total score of 60. The score disbursement is represented in these diagrams.

There are different extremes of combinations from a very even mix:

EVENLY MIXED SPECTRUM

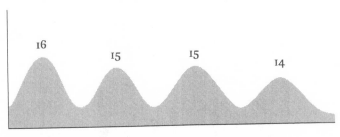

Image 3: Original design by Jessie Lee Perez for *Color By Design*

It stretches from extreme high points with a score of 24, to extreme low points with a score of 6.

HEAVY SIDED SPECTRUM

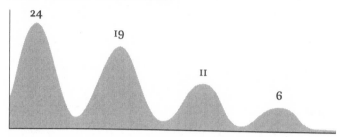

Image 4: Original design by Jessie Lee Perez for *Color By Design*

The struggles and strengths that go with these different blends vary, but are very real. In the case of ADD and other overlays such as compulsive disorders, the signs may lead us to suspect one color yet the true temperament of the person may be another. This may also be true of someone who spends abundant quality time in the presence of God. We may be lead to believe this person has more of a particular color due to the overlain influence of God's character filling a gap.

While there are certainly apparent tells that can be misleading initially, this is the exception, not the norm. It is safe to go with the "tells" when interacting with someone initially and then adapt as you get to know the person more and discover his or her "true colors."

PERSISTENT COLORS

This leads me into the topic of persistency. Some people have questioned if temperament changes over time. Some will even say that theirs has or that it changes based on the role. Carl Jung and some of his predecessors believed that a person's temperament does not change; that a person is born with his or her temperament and I would have to agree mostly.

I think there could be the ever so subtle exception for those whose colors are all nearly tied in the middle scores, leaving it difficult for them to distinguish truly which they favor more on any given day or with regard to particular circumstances, however I believe that with nearly every other spectrum scale, the people really are born into the spectrum to which they will carry through their lives. The spectrum is not a worldview, but rather a way or method in which one thinks. I believe there is merit to the thought of some that their temperaments have changed over time, but not because they've actually changed, but rather because their environment was pulling out certain colors that may or may not have been innately bright in their spectrums.

The most common example for people citing that their temperaments have changed is "when I was in college" as compared to now. Many people believing their colors to have been different while in college are more relating their actions and focus of attention to the color spectrum than their actual strengths and values.

Oftentimes college students are still very much in the phase of self-discovery and rarely have a clear picture of their own strengths during that season. It's also easy for college students to attribute their focus and attention to being akin to needs or values. This may not be the case however.

College is that season when a young person is just getting out and having the freedom to open up to whatever it is that life has to offer and that oftentimes has not been part of their lives at home. Up until that time, many youths were either being told how they were expected to be, or otherwise had some interpretation of what others expected from them. In college, all of a sudden, the expectations imposed by, or interpreted from, others are lifted, and there is an opportunity to be "someone else."

That "someone else" may or may not be truer to that person's self, but the environment is suited to promote one of two spectrum ends; either wide-open carefree tendencies common to Orange where risk is part of the playbook, or buckle-down, focus and withdraw to a more rigid and structured approach common with tendencies found in Gold. While people may range on the intensity of these ends, many people citing a shift in spectrum over time may actually find that after digging into stages of comparison, that perhaps the basis for the colors did not change but the environment drew out more of a color with which he or she did not lead.

There are also times when people draw on a less dominant color in certain environments as it aligns to their role or responsibility. A person could draw on Gold for example if their job required them to be more structured in order to get the job done. This does not mean that the person has shifted in spectrum, but that merely the person is drawing on one of the other colors to accomplish a need. This will be less natural, but we are able to access these other colors as circumstances demand. The more practice we have with them, the more comfortable they can become.

I had mentioned briefly in chapter one that as a youth the orange of my Green-Orange spectrum tended to shine more brightly than my green. This is not because the colors traded places overtime in my temperament, but rather because in my youth I had far fewer opportunities to employ my green. When I look at who I was however, even the things I liked to do for play, it is clear that my green was always there leading. I think that if the people citing spectrum change knew how to evaluate their colors at the level of their truest form, then they also would agree that their colors were present in the same arrangement as they are now and were in college.

CHAPTER 4

Strengths and Style – Finding Your Joy

When considering each color, certain tendencies come to mind, along with these tendencies, certain strengths will be present as well. When we examine these strengths and align them with the needs of each color, we start to see areas where people might excel.

In True Colours sessions, I take the participants through a mock scenario at the end to help drive home the strengths of each color. The Strengths chart lists out a few strengths that are commonly held by each color.

STRENGTHS

ORANGE	BLUE	GREEN	GOLD
Flexibility	Compassion	Big-Picture Thinker (Vision)	Organized
Multitasking	Empathy	Conciseness	Punctual
Positivity	Dependability	Result driven	Follow-Through
Hands-On	Encouraging	Identifying Root Causes	Detail-Oriented
Humor	Democratic	Picking Up on Context Clues	Calculated
Decisiveness	Good Listener	Communicating with Relevance	Planner

Image 5: Original design by Jessie Lee Perez for *Color By Design*

While this is by no means an exhaustive list, it provides some clear themes and examples that can be referenced as you think about people whom you know that clearly have strengths in one of these quadrants.

As we gain in understanding of the strengths people of each color can bring to the table, it will both help us to know where we might best fit, and help us to know where others may fit as well.

For example, the leasing manager of a modern apartment community may be any color, but if we consider the aspects of the job, we may suggest a best-fit temperament style.

A leasing manager interacts daily with the property's tenants, so you would want this person to be personable. Blues are by nature very personable. This role might also be responsible for creating fun activities and arranging offerings to keep the tenants and prospective tenants excited to live and lease at that property. Keeping it fun is most certainly a strength of Orange. So, a Blue-Orange might be a really good fit for this particular position, and a Blue-Orange would also be likely to get satisfaction out of a job that nurtures or caters to his or her strengths.

A Green-Orange may enjoy being an investigator for a time – and might be really good at it. The Green loves to problem solve and looks for scenarios for how all the pieces fit together. The Orange likes the thrill of the adventure and the idea of "winning" if the case is successfully solved. The statement about a Green-Orange liking it "for a time" is because Greens tend to like to build or solve the next big thing, so once it no longer feels like a challenge, a Green might be ready for something new – though if the cases remain interesting, complex and dynamic it could be a satisfying fit for quite a while.

Most ventures, projects, and missions benefit from having people from all colors appropriately applied to areas that will allow them to operate in the strengths and joys of who they are by their very design. It happens however, more typically in volunteer scenarios, that neither the leaders nor those involved in the project or mission can clearly identify the person's innate strengths and thus assign each person to a position or task, which may not be the most beneficial fit. If you take notice, the idea of operating in our "joys" quite often goes hand-in-hand with a person's strengths.

You may have heard someone at some point advise you to choose a career that you enjoy doing – well to a point, this is very true. Many times however, when someone asks us what we like to do or what we enjoy, it is second-tier activities that we think of and with which we respond. Someone might say, "I enjoy fixing cars," or "I enjoy spending time with family," or "I enjoy traveling." While we may enjoy these activities, we may enjoy them for different reasons. When we understand the underlying reasons for the choice, we can more clearly identify not only a few activities we enjoy, but we can assess what types of things might bring us joy even if we've never done them before simply using the characteristics of the activity, and that opens a much greater window of options.

JOYS
ORANGE

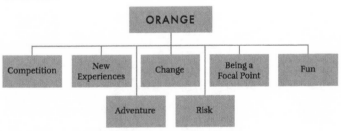

Image 6: Diagram by Jessie Lee Perez for *Color by Design*

When we articulate the actual elements that bring us joy, we can correlate them to the activities we enjoy doing and thereby understand why we enjoy doing those things. Following are some second-tier activities that may correlate with the true joys for Orange.

Travel – it lets them *Adventure* to somewhere different (*Change*) for an opportunity to have *Fun* and have *new experiences*

Hosting a party – it provides the opportunity to be out in front of everyone and to be a *focal point*, while having a forum in which to have *fun*. An Orange is likely to tell someone invited to bring a friend, as meeting new people *mixes it up a bit.*

BLUE

Image 7: Diagram by Jessie Lee Perez for *Color by Design*

Following are some second-tier activities that may correlate with the true joys for Blue. As with Orange, hosting a party may be an activity that bring Blues joy, but you will notice it is for different reasons.

Hosting a party – it provides the opportunity to gather with friends (*relationships*) and *give* others a good time. This would be particularly true if the Blue was hosting the party for someone else (*helping*); bridal shower, baby shower and so on.

Just because gift giving – letting people know they are cared about (*relationships*) or meeting people's needs (real or perceived) (*helping*) by *giving* gifts.

GOLD

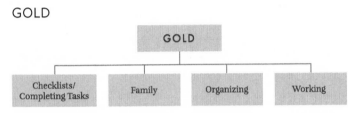

Image 8: Diagram by Jessie Lee Perez for *Color by Design*

Some second-tier activities that correlate with a Gold's joys:

Golds actually enjoy organizing things. If there is a task that needs to get accomplished that involves organizing something, Gold could find great pleasure in that. Not only would the act of organizing be enjoyable, but also the result of completing a task would be extremely satisfying.

Organizing the Pantry/Toolshed – either of these would

provide the feeling of accomplishment and give the person an opportunity to bring order to a particular functional space. This would be particularly satisfying if there was not someone that was likely to come in behind them and leave the area in disarray (maybe an orange family member for example)

Creating the Agenda for the Family vacation – this would tie in the enjoyment of the family unit, while allowing the opportunity to structure the plans (*organize*) all while using the *list* format of a typical agenda.

GREEN

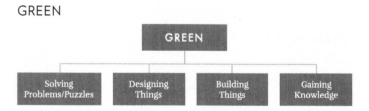

Image 9: Diagram by Jessie Lee Perez for *Color by Design*

Some second-tier activities that correlate with a Green's joys.

Greens really enjoy a challenge. While Oranges are very competitive against others, Greens will find their competitive edge is foremost within themselves. A Green loves intellectual challenges – an opportunity to prove "it can be done." Few Greens believe "impossible" is a word.

Creating a conceptual floor plan for a new building addition – this ties into the concept of *design*, but also an element of *puzzles and problem solving* in trying to optimize the use of the space with the defined needs in place. This also satisfies a joy for *building* things, as mentioned earlier, the actual building doesn't have to be completed by the Green themselves for that person to get satisfaction from it.

Taking a class – Greens are lifetime learners innately and taking a class or classes on a topic that seems interesting or applicable to something the person is doing in life could be a true joy.

CHAPTER 5

Correlating Colors

———

You may notice some common examples of joys between Orange and Blue, but that the motivation driving them is different, as is the case with Green and Gold as well. This is not simply because of the activities I selected as examples, but because Orange and Blue are both "people" driven colors, while Gold and Green are both "process" driven colors. This is a crucial premise in thoroughly understanding people of different colors.

In addition to correlation between People versus Process, there are also pairings along the Risk Tolerance meter. The chart in Image 10 provides a visual depiction of the correlated color relationships.

COLOR CORRELATION CHART

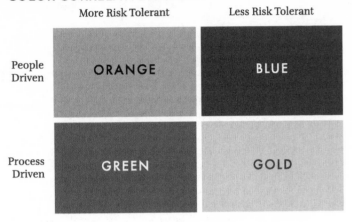

	More Risk Tolerant	Less Risk Tolerant
People Driven	ORANGE	BLUE
Process Driven	GREEN	GOLD

Image 10: Diagram by Jessie Lee Perez for *Color by Design*

RISK TOLERANCE

When considering Risk, several definitions can be applied. Some examples would be as follows:

- Pushing the limits of what has been done before
- Being comfortable with confrontation
- Accepting and moving on from failure
- Confronting change and more

Orange and Green tend to have a much higher risk aptitude than Blue and Gold. Orange sits the highest on the risk tolerance meter, whereas Green is very accepting of risk, but at a calculated level, where it otherwise seems to make sense to achieve their goals. Gold sits the lowest on the risk tolerance meter and really likes to avoid risk, as risk can create high levels of stress for Gold. Blues are a little more risk tolerant in some ways than Gold, but overall still have an aversion to risk, particularly risk that could disrupt levels of harmony among people.

Conflict can also fall into the category of risk to some extent; however, it would be defined in the Color Correlation Chart in a slightly different way. Since Conflict involves People, and Blues are risk-averse people-driven, it seems logical that Blue sits the lowest on the conflict tolerance meter. With Green being process driven, rather than people driven, and having a high risk tolerance, it follows that Green would be the highest on the conflict tolerance meter. This may be better relayed on a linear graph.

CONFLICT TOLERANCE METER

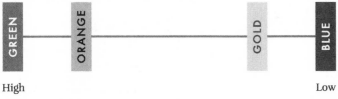

High   Low

Image 11: Meter by Jessie Lee Perez for *Color by Design*

Both Orange and Green are accepting of conflict. Greens may even go as far as to say they are "comfortable" with conflict. Blue and Gold however, are highly conflict averse, and Blue will sometime go to extremes to keep the appearance of a harmonious environment, often bottling up emotions rather than addressing the issue. This, however, can result in inner turmoil or otherwise over spilling a tipping point in an unhealthy way.

PEOPLE DRIVEN
ORANGE

For Orange, the "people" is about the engagement and fun.

BLUE

For Blue the "people" is about the relationship and unity.

PROCESS DRIVEN

The process perspective warrants some additional explanation to help define the specific differences.

GREEN

Greens look at things from a bird's eye view. They tend to take in the big picture of whatever the project, mission or situation may be and draw conclusions based on contextual clues from how the pieces fit together. This creates a sort of map of the landscape, be it a true process-related endeavor, or even a human relational interaction.

This means of ingesting and computing the facts, circumstances, and environment uses pathways to relate meaningful elements from which to base decisions. A Green may not take notice of the independent details if they aren't perceived as important to understanding the bigger picture. Greens are very comfortable with conceptual ideas.

A green sees how all the components fit together and their arrangement to create the whole, making note of patterns and instrumental components.

A visual representation of this concept would be the view of a city from an airplane. The Green sees the layout of the streets, where the buildings are in relation to the park, and patterns in building type, from which assumptions about the city can be drawn.

GREEN VIEW

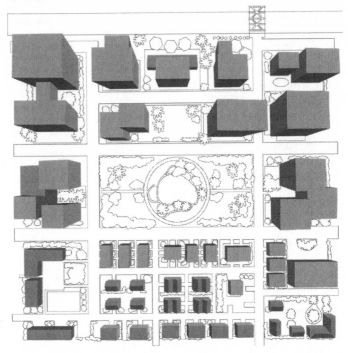

Image 12: Image iStock-635718816 Licensed through iStock by Getty Images

Anyone having ever traveled in an airplane can attest that the view from above is very much different from the view from the ground in the details of everyday life.

GOLD

Golds look at things from the perspective of driving down the street. They need the details, the line by line information. They need to know what comes next and hold an attention to detail focus. Gold can account for the finer details, single unit elements as they add up to the whole. If it's too far ahead or around a corner, Golds may need additional context to bridge the gap. Conceptual detail without the aid of hard facts or visuals may be challenging for a Gold to compute.

Gold lays out the process one component after another and takes into account each detail.

A visual representation of this concept would be a car driving down roadways. The Gold understands house by house, building types, the number of stories, and the demographics of neighborhoods from which assumptions about the city can be drawn using the finite data.

Image 13: Image iStock-583728736 Licensed through iStock by Getty Images

LEVEL OF DETAIL

A Green is not interested in the specifics of detail unless they are instrumental to the decision making point. Even then, it is more likely to be a brief moment of zooming in and then zooming back out to a macro view once sufficient detail has been reached. The Green doesn't like to live in the details.

The Gold very much does live in the details and can give account of every house on every block, the colors of the doors and the components that make them up – figuratively speaking.

A practical example of relating the city view concept to the use of detail in a project would be for community and economic development planning. A Green may relate well to a map highlighting particular community stressors as they result from demographic variance. There may be pertinent facts called out in percentages that would be useful in telling necessary stories for driving conversation and identifying possible solutions to challenges.

Gold may relate better, however, to spreadsheets with all of the specific demographics, community locations, and stressors listed out in columns that can be viewed in patterns, sorted, filtered, viewed independently, and aggregated. Having all of the specific details in view would provide a Gold confidence.

While this is only a single use case, the concept of the application applies to how Greens and Golds approach the thought process of data, and the level of detail expected or desired.

CHAPTER 6

Don't Use Your Color as a Crutch

———

It is not okay for people to excuse inappropriate or inconsiderate behaviors simply because they may have origins in their brightest colors. As explained earlier, each color has both bright sides and shadow sides. We have to be conscious of the potential for these shadows to arise and not use the color spectrum as a pass for not being the best people we can be.

"If it is possible, as far as it depends on you, live at peace with all people" (Romans 12:18, NASB)

It is each one of our own responsibilities to adapt our communication to meet the needs of others. We must value the benefit of our bright colors and use them appropriately. We must also be vigilant of when our innate ways could cause an offense to someone else and minimize this whenever possible.

GREEN CAUTION POINTS

A Green does not get to say, "You are too sensitive, you know that I'm a Green and Greens deliver communication direct and to the point – get used to it." This is a cop out of responsibility. A Green for example may need to be conscious not to respond sarcastically when he or she feels threatened or confronted. Greens may also find that when they try to joke with people, in ways others may find well received, that the response is negative and the joke may even come across hurtful. Being intentional and cognizant of others' responses will help a Green identify certain communication and delivery techniques that may be best avoided or used sparsely and with the utmost care. Greens can help overcome stigmas resulting from directness by taking opportunities to show others that they matter; listen longer, more attentively, ask a question in response to let the people know you have heard them, look them in the eye. These are just a few examples of intentional actions that can be applied.

GOLD CAUTION POINTS

Golds need to be cautious not to assume that all people see things exactly the same way as they do, or are otherwise wrong. While things may seem very black and white to a Gold, it is important to remember that the other colors see through multiple shades of gray, some more than others. So while a choice or action may seem like an implausible answer to a Gold, people of other colors may not see that perspective with such clarity – for better or worse.

Golds also have certain automatic tendencies when they feel threatened. They need to remember that name calling and bullying behavior is not an acceptable response when their expectations are not met. While not all Golds find this a struggle, it is a shadow that tends to arise in Golds more than in other colors. A litmus test to identify if this may be a factor in how a Gold handles conflict could be to reflect on the ability to separate the person doing the action from the action done in the moment when tensions are elevated. If the direct response is a blow to the character of the person, rather than addressing the situation, then bullying is likely a shadow that needs to be monitored and addressed.

ORANGE CAUTION POINTS

Oranges need to recognize that not everyone is as flexible or as open to change as an Orange. An Orange needs to honor commitments made and respect the time of others. Being late to engagements may not be as "okay" as it may seem, and others may really take offense to last minute changes of plans or missed commitments. Oranges also may need to be intentional to minimize overt responses to undesirable circumstances or confrontational behavior. It is not acceptable to use your color as an excuse to become physically or verbally explosive when things are opposing you (real or perceived). Oranges need to keep a check on their focus as well, as it is easy for an Orange to get caught up in the "it's all about me" mentality without realizing it. This may come out in a variety of ways, but reflecting on time usage will often help an Orange evaluate if he or she is putting an excessive amount of attention on him or herself. Simply ask, "What is my time used doing, and what is my motivation for that usage?"

BLUE CAUTION POINTS

A common shadow for Blues is the tendency to talk around the subject. Blues are great storytellers, but in such are not always great at getting to the point. This can leave ambiguity and opens the door to misunderstanding by and frustrations of others. Blues also need to be self-aware that they do not allow themselves to become negatively emotionally driven when threatened (again, real or perceived) or when hurt. This could result in a Bitter Blue. Bitter Blues have roots of undealt with unforgiveness in their past; areas when they have been offended and in true-to-Blue fashion, suppressed the pain as to not further disrupt the relationships or create additional conflict.

Another tendency of hurt Blues is to cut off completely people when they feel they have been wronged more than a couple times. This could occasionally result in a Blue cutting off entire groups, or perceived categories, of people that a Blue associates to the person or people responsible for the hurt.

Blues may also have to guard against the draw to engage in gossip. A Blue is always up for a good story, but when the story crosses into gossip, it should be avoided. A good check to see if something is gossip is if the information provided is not publicly shared by the person involved and there is no action or intervention the person receiving the information can take to positively impact the other person's situation.

LEARNING FROM OUR SHADOWS

While each color has its shadows, when we recognize our capability for shadows, we can begin to identify times when we may operate in these shadows and take the initiative to learn from those moments and grow beyond the natural responses typical to each color. While conflict will arise, it is important to approach and handle it in a healthy and mature way.

We each have an important role to play in this.

There are other areas of shadows as well that are those innate outward facing actions and demeanors that would suggest negative behavior when interpreted by another color. These may still be mitigated to an extent, but community growth in the understanding of each other will aid in misapplied impressions. In other words, the more people who speak color, the fewer conflicts we will encounter from color-related misunderstandings.

Examples of these shadows (as perceived by others):

- Orange – May come across as a show-off
- Blue – May come across as emotional
- Gold – May come across as rigid
- Green – May come across as arrogant

The people themselves may see the same behavior as:

- Orange – fun/lively
- Blue – caring/concerned
- Gold – structured/responsible
- Green – competent/learned

It is clear that simple perspective can completely derail interactions if we are not knowledgeable about each other's colors. It is also important to be knowledgeable about our own tendencies that operate within us with respect to our colors to ensure we are not dismissing unacceptable behavior with the excuse of color.

CHAPTER 7

Me First, Servant Leadership

Me First – This may not sound like something you would expect to hear paired with a topic on servant leadership, but it is a necessary preliminary component. We have to understand our own motivations in order to bring ourselves to a place where we can be sure our motivation is in love for others instead of selfish need.

Blues, for example, have an innate aptitude for compassion and are usually the first to volunteer to help out. Blues also, among other needs, have the need to feel appreciated. There is nothing wrong with these things (I don't think there's anyone who wouldn't like to be appreciated). A matter of the heart could creep up however if a Blue is driven to do helpful and nice things for the purpose of filling the need of being appreciated rather than for the purpose of serving others. A fine line would be unnoticeably crossed as it were viewed by others. Only the Blue him or herself would be able to identify this. The outer action could appear very much the same.

It's time for some self-evaluation.

If you find that you have been serving as an indirect means of self-service, there is no need to beat yourself up about it, simply turn it over to God. Invite Him in to check your heart, ask Him to forgive you for misaligning your gifts, and ask Him to help you lead with His love for the sake of others. Through it, you will be satisfied. It will look much the same on the outside, but the motivation will be genuine, which will actually bring greater satisfaction. It will no longer be validated by the response of others, but by the will and love of God.

Each color has areas that should be subject to self-evaluation to ensure we are true to the purpose of God in serving others.

Golds are fantastic at following up on the details. Each "i" is dotted and "t" is crossed when a Gold is responsible for the task. Excellence is certainly something to stretch to achieve. Gold, however, may develop a certain idea of what excellence looks like in an area and become inflexible to seeing the excellence in others if the process or method of the others does not look like what the Gold has decided excellence looks like.

I know that was a heavy statement, but go back and read it again if you must, as this could be a profoundly chain-breaking revelation if it is something that you exhibit.

There is an inner-evaluation opportunity for bright Golds to continuously check to see if they have set expectations simply based on the way he or she would do it or if the expectation for excellence is genuinely about hitting the mark for excellence rather than the process or method fitting into the expected formula for achieving it.

Another area for Golds to self-monitor is for risk of falling into a comfort zone. Golds, of all colors, really prefer to dwell in a comfort zone. When things are routine and predictable, then stress is down and there is a familiarity that provides a cushion of comfort. However, when we commit our lives to God, He wants us to grow, and growing requires stretching. This will take us out of our comfort zone into unfamiliar territory.

If we truly want to operate in excellence, we need to understand that excellence is a moving line, not a fixed one. That which was excellent 10 years ago will not be the mark we are still trying to reach today. We should have far superseded that mark. Golds need to be cautious not to get stuck thinking that "this is the way it has always been and it was excellent then, so it is still excellent." Change is hard for Golds, but it is truly the only way to maintain excellence.

While Oranges have no problem with change (they actually like it), Oranges are not exempt from the need for self-evaluation of motives. An Orange may volunteer for activities or to lead people, groups, or projects.

The appearance could suggest someone who has bravely stepped up to lead. Moreover, while there may be a very good intention behind an Orange stepping out in front, there also is a need and joy for Oranges to feel like they are the center of attention. There is a need for people willing to lead, but if the motivation is fueled by wanting to feel important or for the attention of a crowd, then there is a heart issue that needs to be addressed. I've heard it said that if someone is eager to lead, then he or she probably isn't ready for it. It is those that realize the responsibility of the role of leadership that may be willing if called, but not eager, that will be able to lead with the stability necessary and from the right perspective and motivations.

Greens also have great leadership abilities. They are innately able to see the greater vision and cast vision. Greens however don't innately consider the people side. While a Green may have all of the of the process points worked out and defined, a Green may not have taken the initiative to consider how the project, plan or task might impact others involved.

Does the vision require change from others? How will those involved respond to the need to change? How could this be made easier for them? Do those involved understand the vision? Is a plan to be executed without including the buy in from others?

It is easy to push away people when they haven't been considered and a plan that involves them has been completely establish surrounding the components of process and execution. People are crucial components to optimizing success. When a Green takes the time to stop and remember that the people part is something that needs intentional attention, not only will people involved feel more appreciated, but also the project in whole will ultimately be more successful.

When we take the time to remember our natural tendencies and put intentional consideration on the areas that would bring shadows into the effort we undertake, giving time for a little self-evaluation, then we will ultimately serve better and be better leaders.

An important job as leaders is to help those we lead to grow and become the best they can be. If we have not first done some self-evaluation to determine areas of adjustment or attention needed within ourselves based on the simple makeup of who we are, then how can we be expected to effectively help others do the same? There is a rebuke in the book of Luke, 6:42 that says, "...first take the log out of your own eye, then you will see clearly to take the speck out of your brother's eye" (NASB). This offers a great visual to the importance of adopting a Me First perspective while approaching the topic of Servant Leadership.

CHAPTER 8

Loving in Color

We are called upon to love one another. In this, we need to love people for who they are and not for whom we think they should be. Each and every person has value and each and every person has an intentional wiring that leads him or her to think in a particular manner as explained through the color spectrum.

When we truly love someone, we are willing to sacrifice for that person. Jesus Christ said, "Greater love hath no man but this, that a man lay down his life for his friends" (John 15:13 KJV). We are rarely called to lay down our lives. But, can we at least lay down our colors for a time?

May I ask you – whose responsibility is it to speak someone else's color?

It is everyone's responsibility to speak the other person's

color. This is to act in love. Too often we get stuck in our own ways and use the excuse, "this is just who I am." While that may be true, once we really know who we are and can understand others as well, it becomes each of our responsibility to speak the other person's color.

It is very often that misunderstandings and offenses come because people are oblivious to the expectations and needs of others.

If only we would regularly ask ourselves, "what do others need to be the best they can be, and how can I help give that to them?"

When we see people for who they truly are and recognize their value and strengths, we are better able to love them. If we can remove the outer appearance of attitudes, perceived motivations, and misunderstandings, we will be prepared to put actions and intentions into operation.

CHAPTER 9

Don't Fake It Until You Make It

———

There are two schools of thought on strengths and weaknesses. The earlier position was once you know your strengths and weaknesses, you can pour in time and effort into trying to improve your weaknesses and create better balance. The latter, and the one to which I prefer to subscribe, is that once you know your strengths and weaknesses, recognize your weaknesses, but give the attention and time to honing and perfecting your strengths.

There is nothing wrong with improving areas of weakness along the way, but we can't force our weaknesses into strengths. While I would say there is definitely a place for "fake it until you make it", being yourself is not the place for that. Sometimes people try to compensate for their weaknesses in ways that come across as fake, over-the-top, arrogant, or just outright mean.

I think many people who emit one or more of these impressions are doing so to try to be someone they were never designed to be, or are too wrapped up in trying to "fake their weaknesses into strengths" that they miss the strengths they do have. If they could recognize their strengths and the value that they can bring to the table through those strengths, and simply be content in their weaknesses, then it opens up a level of freedom that will maximize their opportunity for success.

One of the best ways to be content in oneself is in surrender of self. The only one safely able to receive the surrender is God. As we enter into a relationship with Him and allow ourselves to surrender to Him, we gain a new level of confidence in who we are. Not only will we gain more confidence in our strengths, but also instead of haughty confidence, it will be a purposeful confidence. We will also have a confidence in our weaknesses, not because they have become strengths, but because God holds us and will divinely fill in the gap in any situation to which He calls us. And, if He does not call us to a situation then we don't need to be there anyway and won't need to depend on our own areas of weakness. There will most certainly be opportunities to partner with a person having strengths in those areas.

CHAPTER 10

Building Relation-ships and Finding Yourself in God

When we are real with God, having a relationship with Him is much like having a relationship with another person. In doing so, we are likely to approach our relationship with Him in a similar manner as we would a relationship with another person.

There are different stages to developing a relationship. The initial stage is the introduction. This is followed by the meet-and-greet. Then comes the light friendship. After that, if parties are both open to allow a furthering of the relationship, it becomes a deep fellowship (this is not defined as a romantic relationship, and this step usually develops without conscious intention if it does happen).

This is where the parties involved engage in deeper, personal, and sensitive communication, share time spent in a focus on each other and mutual interests, and growth can be developed. In the natural realm, a level of relationship called romantic relationship could be pursued following a deep fellowship for two people of the opposite sex who feel they are led by God to commit each of their lives to the other under the covenant of marriage. We may think that this level does not apply to a relationship with God, but it most certainly does. God describes His intended relationship with His church through the Bible as the bride and the bridegroom. He speaks of the marriage supper and the day "she," the church, will be presented free of stain or blemish (Ephesians 5:27).

Some have walked into this level of relationship with God and have experienced the depth of satisfaction that accompanies it. Like many person to person relationships that enter into this level however, daily life continues to demand attention and there is a temptation to drift from the passion that connects the two and become complacent in the relationship. This is a dangerous shift and needs to be addressed. Tactics can be put in place to keep from drifting in this direction, but like any romantic relationship, like any marriage, it will take intentional effort. Let's get into each section and discuss the application of each color to these different levels of relationship.

LEVELS OF RELATIONSHIP
THE INTRODUCTION

The Introduction is when people first meet. This includes the first impression as well as the initial context perceived about a person's character.

MEET-AND-GREET

The Meet-and-Greet is when people enter into light conversation, social encounters, and pleasantries. Many people may have a number of relationships that stay in this phase. These people see each other in the grocery store and recognize each other. They may or may not remember the other person's name as they exchange a few pleasantries, ask high level, open-ended questions like "how's the family?" or some vague status question about a known personal fact.

LIGHT FRIENDSHIP

The Light Friendship is when people engage in social enjoyment together and are familiar at some level with the other person's personal life. This could be work buddies, moms who get their kids together outside of the children's sporting events, friends from school/college, or other connections that develop in which people continue to gather and engage for mutual enjoyment.

DEEP FELLOWSHIP

The Deep Fellowship is when people come into relationships with levels of confidence. They feel a level of freedom to share deeper thoughts, feelings, ideas, and dreams/visions without feeling a concern of being ostracized, judged or rejected. These are the relationships that can offer a level of comfort even in those times of silence.

ROMANTIC

The Romantic level is when people enter into personal intimacy with each other. This may be at an emotional level, a physical level, or both. It involves shared time of private communion that would be uncomfortably held if additional people were present.

GOLD IN RELATIONSHIP

As mentioned previously, when a Gold first meets someone, there is a cautious distance. Gold does not tend to jump in and let down his or her guard upon initial introduction. This applies no differently to a relationship with God. A new believer will often, upon making that important decision to follow God and ask Jesus to be his or her Lord and Savior, want to stay in that position of "I'm saved, now what?" (and I will note that this refers to a relationship begun with an adult person, as children will exhibit many of the same outward similarities, but have a level of faith that makes them more open to trust even those they don't know). Gold will operate with a level of caution to release control and walk into a trust relationship. A Gold may be willing to linger in the meet-and-greet place as he or she begins to learn the character of the God they've just welcomed as Savior. The meet-and-greet level would be the place where the person doesn't get too personal with topics of conversation and may engage during mutual activities but does not specifically go out with the explicit purpose of doing something with the other person. Gold may take a similar approach to building a relationship with God. The person may engage lightly and avoid getting too personal and certainly not vulnerable, while in the initial stages with God. Once the person has had enough evidence that God is who He claims to be and can be trusted with love and wants the best for him or her, then there is greater openness to move into a deeper level of relationship. Once in a deeper fellowship, the Gold will respond with great loyalty.

BLUE IN RELATIONSHIP

A Blue's life is built for relationship, so it is unsurprising that a Blue would be much more welcoming to jump into a level of relationship beyond the initial introduction very quickly. If a Blue feels any kind of connection, that person may move right past the meet-and-greet phase almost straight into the light friend phase. If that goes well and the connection is maintained a Blue would often be willing to go into a deeper Fellowship, so long as trust is not broken. A bruised or battered Blue is another story however. A Bitter Blue, may result if the offenses are severe enough and not dealt with. As you recall I mentioned earlier that a Blue will forgive once, twice, but three times, you're out – well, a Blue who has had his or her trust broken will not likely go to any level with the other person. There is certainly a potential for the same aversion to apply to a Blue's relationship with God as well. While there is a potential that a Blue could feel as though he or she has been wronged by God, there is a more common potential that the role of God in the person's life, or as explained to the person, is tainted by broken trust by a person in that role.

For example, God is described often as a father. To many this conveys a sense of protection, love and leadership, but to a Blue who was hurt by his or her father (emotionally, physically, abandonment, etc.), the role of a father leaves a sense of distrust and the number of remaining, undealt with emotions. This could make moving past the stage of meet-and-greet with God a scary and potentially dreadful risk. The desire to become vulnerable before God or dependent on Him could have the person wanting to turn and run. But, that is where a relationship with God is different. God will meet us where we are, and while He always wants us to go deeper, He will not force us to do so. If we are willing, He will deal with our hesitancy in the stage where we are and will draw us into the necessary level of healing and trust that will allow us to overcome those hurts and move to the next level. The deeper we are willing to go with Him, the deeper He will be able to work the pain and hurt out of us, setting us free to love and trust in ways we may have felt we would never again be able to do. There is an abundance of health and freedom in the surrender that comes with a deep relationship with God, that is true regardless of your color.

The same types of hindrances to truly living in the best relationship with God can occur with the role of God as husband/bridegroom, King, Lord, master, and numerous other titles. If a Blue has been hurt from multiple sources, it may take getting through each one individually to truly feel equipped to trust God in that deep fellowship or covenant relationship. Once a Blue can reconcile his or her relationship with God, that person will find a freedom in other strained person-to-person relationships as well.

ORANGE IN RELATIONSHIP

An Orange may move quickly to the stage of light friendship, but should be cautioned not to get too comfortable there. An Orange has a driver for freedom and embraces change, so there is an aversion to the idea of being committed or being locked into any particular relationship.

Oranges like to have fun and not miss out on anything, so there is a dangerous tendency to want to play with relationships at a deep enough level to get something from them, but not too deep to be tied down or responsible for them. An Orange may be more likely than other colors to resist marriage for fear of that commitment.

The same principles would hold true with his or her relationship with God. An Orange may be zealous and excited about the relationship initially and jump right in. The level of depth and commitment could waiver however, as a deep relationship with God means letting go of the relationship with the world and an Orange may struggle more than any other color with making this commitment to choose one. The hope that he or she can just ride the line and try to get the best of both would be very common for an Orange. This however is a losing angle no matter how it's played.

"[No one] can serve two masters for either he will hate one, and love the other, or else he will hold to one, and despise the other. [You] cannot serve God and man" (Luke 16:13, NASB).

An Orange will have a very serious decision to move into a deep relationship and covenant with God, but that decision becomes a lot easier when he or she recognizes it as the opportunity it is.

There is a song, which verses I think will resonate well with an Orange:

"It's got to be more like falling in love
Than something to believe in
More like losing my heart
Than giving my allegiance
Give me rules
I will break them
Show me lines
I will cross them
I need more than a truth to believe
I need truth that lives, moves, and breathes
To sweep me off my feet"
(GRAY, J. & INGRAM, J, MORE LIKE FALLING IN LOVE)

The song goes on from there, but you get the point. For Orange, committing to come into that awesome relationship is going to be about the prospective adopted.

GREEN IN RELATIONSHIP

Green's aren't usually fast to make friends but a Green might be willing to move right along through the stages if it makes sense. If a Green has a plan or purpose for the relationship, then the Green may progress into a simple step process to the appropriate stage for the intent of that relationship.

Greens are often misunderstood, so for a Green who has experienced levels of shunning from people throughout life, that person will tend to adopt a cautious and methodical decision making process for when to let people in and how deep. A Green may even consciously recognize when he or she allows someone to go from one stage to the next.

This may come across harsh and ingenuine, but I assure you it is not. It is simply a different way of approaching a relationship. A Green can love just as deeply as a Blue, or any other color for that matter, it just may be surrounded with a different way of getting there or different responses if someone does "wrong."

Just as we've seen with the other colors, a Green will often approach his or her relationship with God in a similar fashion to that taken with relationships with people. A Green may question: "What is the purpose of this relationship?" "What are all the options?" and "Why should I trust God?" If the answer to these questions is satisfactorily met for the Green, then that person is likely to start into the relationship and progress to the next stage, possibly pausing to learn and then ask the "why's," whether consciously or not, before moving to the next stage. As God proves Himself to a Green in each stage however, he or she will continue on as the person continues to see the value, especially as growth is realized in the person's life.

God has a plan for each of us. As we understand ourselves and how we are designed, we can observe and understand our natural tendencies and responses in different situations. Once we recognize this, we can more successfully walk in healthy and productive relationships both with God and in connection with others.

CHAPTER 11

Final Thoughts

———

When we speak color we not only open the doors to improved communication and relationships, but we also open the opportunity walk in unity like never before. True Colours gives the personal understanding, self-awareness and knowledge of others that is sure to spur growth and collaboration if put into action. While this is a fantastic tool for maturing teams, and personal and professional growth, it is ultimate something that is so much greater. Imagine a world where we can truly understand each other regardless of our language, age, or outer appearance – where we no longer feel alone with no one that understands us – where we can feel confident to know that we are made like this on purpose and for a purpose. In addition, through this we now have the ability to value each other's strengths in areas that maybe we never could before. We can now walk in community. It's not about identifying our differences, it's about appreciating the value that the differences add to the community – You, I, We, create the community and every one of us is an indispensable part of the total picture. When we come together in color, we become the solution for our family, for our community, for our world.

Don't let your enterprise, your family, and your nation, fail because diversity was superficial, or because it was a wedge instead of the unifier – adopt a culture of color. Learn to speak color today and become an agent for unity.

Further Readings and Bibliography

—

FURTHER READINGS

If you want to further explore what it means to enter into a relationship with God the Father, through a relationship with Jesus Christ the Son, and for who He is, visit FreedomHI.org.

Additional reading on understanding your strengths can be found in *Strengths Finder* by Tom Rath, which is a great compliment to True Colours.

For more focused reading on understanding those you love in your life, *5 Love Languages* by Gary Chapman is a valuable resource.

Additional techniques for successful communication, both professionally and personally, can be found in *Crucial Conversations* by Patterson, Grenny, McMillan and Switzler.

BIBLIOGRAPHY

Giblin, Les. How to Have Confidence and Power in Dealing with People. New York: Prentice Hall Press, 1956.

Gray, J. & Ingram, J. Lyrics to "More Like Falling in Love." *Everything Sad is Coming Untrue* [Album], Centricity Music, 2009.

Biblical references come from the New American Standard Bible (NASB) and King James Version (KJV) [as indicated]

True Colours is a temperament assessment and training workshop crafted by Christine Gardener, as derived from the original work of True Colors (1978) by Don Lowery, and based on the work of Myers-Briggs.

About the Author

JESSIE LEE PEREZ has worked or served in sixteen foreign nations. A seasoned business analyst with a strategic mindset and a flare for adventure, she has operated in such industries as international logistics, NASA atmospheric sciences, and cancer services. Jessie holds a degree in global business from Regent University, is a certified facilitator of True Colours workshops and training, and is passionate about driving transformation in individuals and communities through the ability to speak color. She lives in Nashville, Tennessee, with her family.

NOTES

NOTES

NOTES

NOTES

NOTES

Made in the USA
Lexington, KY
27 March 2018